《走进新疆》丛书（第三辑）

主编：刘长明

天 上 人 间

——丝绸之路之谜

Heavenly World

——Secrets Of The Silk Road

绿 阳　文昊 编

by Lu Yang　Wen Hao

新疆美术摄影出版社
新疆电子音像出版社

图书在版编目(CIP)数据

　　天上人间／绿阳,文昊主编.—乌鲁木齐:新疆美术
摄影出版社;新疆电子音像出版社,2008.12
　ISBN 978-7-80744-516-6

　Ⅰ.天… Ⅱ.①绿…②文… Ⅲ.丝绸之路—简介 Ⅳ.
K928.6

中国版本图书馆 CIP 数据核字(2009)第 000145 号

《走进新疆》丛书(第三辑)
主　编　　刘长明

天上人间——丝绸之路之谜

编　　者	绿　阳　　文　昊
图片摄影	文　昊　　晏　先
	文　焱　　温　倩
	张永江　　向　京
英文翻译	迪娜·迪里木拉提
责任编辑	吴晓霞
装帧设计	李瑞芳

出　　版	新疆美术摄影出版社
	新疆电子音像出版社
	(乌鲁木齐市西虹西路 36 号　830000)
发　　行	新华书店
印　　刷	海洋彩印有限公司
开　　本	787mm×1092mm　　1/24
印　　张	4.5
字　　数	12 千字　　138 幅图片
版　　次	2008 年 12 月第 1 版
印　　次	2009 年 1 月第 1 次印刷
书　　号	ISBN 978-7-80744-516-6
定　　价	58.00 元

SECRETS OF
THE SILK ROAD
领略西域风情
感悟西域风光
天上人间

Heavenly World

——Secrets Of The Silk Road

目录

Contents 目录

Heavenly World

——Secrets Of The Silk Road

SECRETS OF
THE SILK ROAD

领略西域风情
感悟西域风光

天上人间

亚历山大大帝、成吉思汗蒙古武士、马可·波罗、玄奘和无数商旅们，曾经沿着这条丝绸之路寻找着他们的理想、珍爱和财富。

丝绸之路是一条纵横交错蜿蜒曲折的贸易之路，是由中国汉武帝两次派遣张骞出使西域历经艰辛，几经磨难开辟的。丝绸之路主要部分是在新疆。新疆是中国土地面积最大的省份。围绕着塔克拉玛干沙漠，丝绸之路分为南北两条途径。一条沿昆仑山北麓经新疆翻越葱岭南部经阿富汗、伊朗诸国抵达地中海或南至印度，此为南道；一条沿天山南麓经新疆翻越葱岭经大宛、康居、奄蔡(里海)抵达罗马，此为北道。

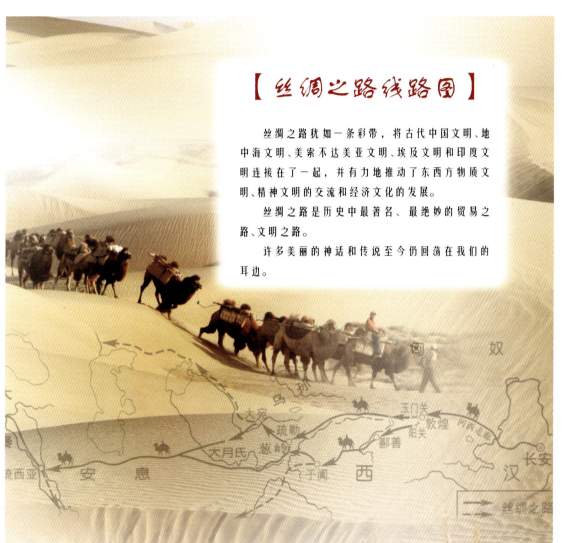

【丝绸之路线路图】

丝绸之路犹如一条彩带，将古代中国文明、地中海文明、美索不达米亚文明、埃及文明和印度文明连接在了一起，并有力地推动了东西方物质文明、精神文明的交流和经济文化的发展。

丝绸之路是历史中最著名、最绝妙的贸易之路、文明之路。

许多美丽的神话和传说至今仍回荡在我们的耳边。

匈奴

乌孙

玉门关

大宛

疏勒 敦煌 河西走廊

大月氏 葱岭 鄯善

西 汉 长安

条西亚 安 息 于阗

丝绸之路

【 沙　　漠 】

塔克拉玛干沙漠是继撒哈拉沙漠之后的世界第二大流动沙漠。

几十个世纪以来,塔克拉玛干沙漠一直被称为"死亡之海",它像一个胃口极大的野兽,吞食了城市和新疆的古老文明,让它们永远地埋在沙海深处。

20世纪初,瑞典著名的探险家斯文·赫定在此发现了楼兰故城。

它曾今是中国神秘的西域——新疆36个繁荣昌盛的王国之一。

摄影:文昊

【楼 兰】

约在 4 世纪中叶，位于罗布泊腹地的楼兰城被神秘废弃，以后漫成一片茫茫沙海。

20世纪初，瑞典探险家斯文·赫定在中国神秘的西域发现了新疆 36 个繁荣昌盛的王国之一楼兰故城。

在对楼兰故城考古发现中，最珍贵的就是保存完美的女性木乃伊——"楼兰美女"。

用现代科学技术再现女性木乃伊的面貌，它就是现在我们所熟知的"楼兰美女"。

人们在沙漠中不仅发现了废墟，而且还发现了壮观的石化林和数千株硅酸树。

【塔里木河】

人们为抵御沙丘的移动,种植了有着非凡生命力的植物去应对天气变化,以抵御干旱、洪水和凶猛的沙尘暴的袭击。

然而,人类还是无法同恶劣的自然环境相抗衡。

结果无情的沙漠仍旧在不断扩大。

由于气候的变化,导致了全球气候变暖,塔克拉玛干沙漠的周边环境条件恶化。山脉的冰川缩小,雪线上升,土地减少并且越发沙化。

与多数沙漠不同的是,塔克拉玛干沙漠有多条河流流入。

这些河流将冰山雪水引至沙漠。

塔里木河是有名的沙漠之河,雪水流入其支流,随之进入沙漠消失在沙海中。曲折蜿蜒的小河流过茫茫沙漠创造了罗布泊。

【罗布人村寨】

　　金色的胡杨和鱼生活在塔里木河的周围。世代生活在塔里木河下游和罗布泊周围低洼的维吾尔罗布人，是新疆古老的土著居民。传统的罗布人不种五谷，不牧牲畜，惟以小舟捕鱼为生。一片繁叶茂盛的胡杨林，一座古朴安逸的小草屋，一汪宁静悠然的小海子，再加上一只心爱的卡盆，构成了罗布人村寨最为质朴的生活图景。

摄影：文焱

SECRETS OF
THE SILK ROAD

领略西域风情
感悟西域风光

天上人间

摄影:温倩

摄影:温倩

摄影:温倩

SECRETS OF
THE SILK ROAD

领略西域风情
感悟西域风光

天上人间

摄影:文焱

【吐鲁番】

吐鲁番盆地,也被称为火洲,在中国乃至全世界是最热的地区之一。

东接河西走廊,西接塔里木盆地,使吐鲁番在丝绸之路中战略意义尤为重要。

尽管该地气温很高,缺雨少水,但吐鲁番的农业迅速发展。

这片美丽富饶的土地正在受到来自周围塔克拉玛干沙漠的日益扩大而带来的威胁。

摄影:晏先

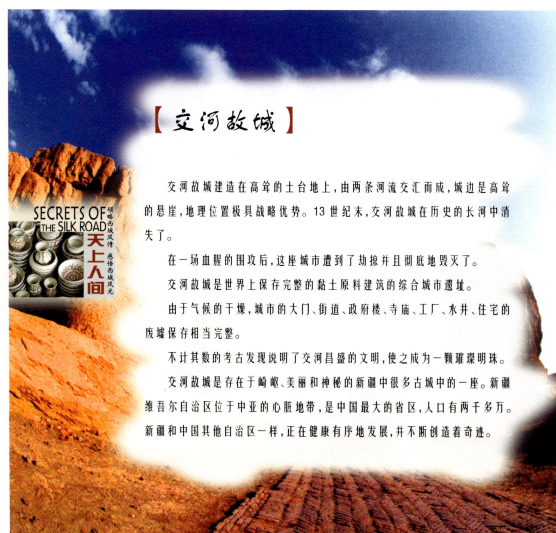

【交河故城】

交河故城建造在高耸的土台地上，由两条河流交汇而成，城边是高耸的悬崖，地理位置极具战略优势。13世纪末，交河故城在历史的长河中消失了。

在一场血腥的围攻后，这座城市遭到了劫掠并且彻底地毁灭了。

交河故城是世界上保存完整的黏土原料建筑的综合城市遗址。

由于气候的干燥，城市的大门、街道、政府楼、寺庙、工厂、水井、住宅的废墟保存相当完整。

不计其数的考古发现说明了交河昌盛的文明，使之成为一颗璀璨明珠。

交河故城是存在于崎岖、美丽和神秘的新疆中很多古城中的一座。新疆维吾尔自治区位于中亚的心脏地带，是中国最大的省区，人口有两千多万。新疆和中国其他自治区一样，正在健康有序地发展，并不断创造着奇迹。

【坎儿井】

　　坎儿井中国古代3大工程之一，可以与长城和京杭大运河相媲美。

　　坎儿井，这一独一无二、庞大的地下水利系统，汇聚了冰山雪峰之雪水和地下水形成了长达5000千米的灌溉饮用暗渠，涵养了世代居民和广大农田。这是生活在这里的各族人民勤劳与智慧的结晶。

　　这个系统确保了地下水的流量、冰凉和纯净，不会被炎热的气温和强烈的风所蒸发及空气污染。

　　这项巧夺天工的工程有将近2000年的历史，是它繁荣了吐鲁番的农业文明，它将与世长存。

摄影：文焱

13

【 吐峪沟居民 】 摄影:晏先

当宣礼员开始宣礼时,回音穿越了草木繁茂的山谷和古城。人们采摘吐鲁番有名的水果——葡萄,在葡萄架下庆祝着收获,歌舞升平,这是维吾尔人的传统活动,又称作麦西来甫。

吐鲁番是东西文化荟萃之地,萨满教、佛教、伊斯兰教等多种宗教在这里融合。在吐峪沟的居民风俗文化中,反映了该地区历史文化的深厚积淀。

SECRETS OF
THE SILK ROAD
领略西域风情 感悟西域风光
天上人间

这儿有大小麦西来甫,通常大型的麦西来甫在婚礼、重要的节日或者有贵客来临时举行。

每个人都会穿上五彩缤纷的传统服装陶醉在麦西来甫所带来的欢乐中。

他们不仅种植甜美可口的葡萄,而且为全世界喜欢葡萄酒的人酿制上等的葡萄酒。

新鲜的葡萄同样也会被晾干,晾葡萄的地方称作晾房。

晾房为两层黏土土块结构,墙上留有许多的小洞,便于炎热的沙漠空气的流通来风干葡萄。

这个过程大概需要40天左右,保护了葡萄的叶绿素不被流失和葡萄的自然色泽。

绿色的、紫色的葡萄干十分精美。

SECRETS OF
THE SILK ROAD

领略西域风情
感悟西域风光

天上人间

摄影:向京

摄影：向京

摄影：翟克伦

【 葡萄种植 】

　　吐鲁番是葡萄的故乡，葡萄是吐鲁番的象征，走进吐鲁番就是走进了葡萄的世界。葡萄编织着吐鲁番人的生活，装扮着吐鲁番人的生活环境。葡萄是吐鲁番的灵魂。

　　这里的居民在吐鲁番独有的气候环境中，凭着他们多年的经验和智慧，将享誉世界的葡萄充分利用，使今天的人们可以品尝到葡萄的甘甜醇美。

【苏公塔】

在离吐鲁番市中心不远处我们发现了苏公塔。

塔高 37 米，由泥砖和木头建成。塔由 15 种不同风格的图案装饰，具有浓郁的伊斯兰艺术特色。

苏公塔建于 1778 年，又叫额敏塔，额敏和卓恩塔。相传是吐鲁番郡王苏来曼为纪念和表彰其父额敏和卓平定准噶尔贵族叛乱所建树的赫赫战功而修建的，是新疆现今最大的古塔。

SECRETS OF
THE SILK ROAD
领略西域风情
感悟西域风光
天上人间

摄影：文焱

【烽火台】

隐藏在火焰山里的是柏孜克里克千佛洞。

它们已经被盗墓者、抢劫者和无道失义的考古者多次破坏和劫掠。他们揭走无价的佛教壁画。

自1982年起,这里的政府和考古、文物工作者已经开始注意保护这些历史遗迹。

当凶猛的风继续刮过贫瘠的沙漠,我们跟随着大篷车经过了用土砖和木头以及混杂着一些芦苇草建成的烽火台。

这些孤零零的烽火台是古代中国人民的杰作,是长城的延伸。现在这些废墟是丝绸之路上的一个个景点。

帝王的烽火台是一个提前报警系统,随时提醒驻防军队注意抵御敌人的进攻。

在古代,在崎岖不平的漫长道路上,古人用泥土和芦苇建造了无数个烽火台。用烟火信息来提醒驻防军防御敌军,使生活在这片土地上的人们尽可能地保护自己。

摄影:晏先

SECRETS OF
THE SILK ROAD

领略西域风情
感悟西域风光

天上人间

摄影：文焱

【维吾尔人的生活】

木卡姆是新疆的音乐。

木卡姆是维吾尔文化的血液。

它表现了维吾尔人豪放、活泼的个性和文化。

原始的、狂热的木卡姆表演是很多庆祝活动上的一部分。

木卡姆音乐是新疆的灵魂，在各种麦西来甫活动中是缺一不可的。

维吾尔族男女喜欢戴美丽的绣花帽。

女子们穿上多彩的丝绸裙，并且把头发梳成很多条辫子。

摄影:温倩

　　维吾尔人见面打招呼时不相互握手，但会将右手放在各自的胸前说："希望你有一个美好的生活。"当见到尊贵长者或客人，他们将两只手交叉放在胸前打招呼。

　　女性们之间见面时有她们自己的礼仪，她们互相拥抱并触碰对方的脸颊，同时说"希望你有一个美好生活"。

SECRETS OF
THE SILK ROAD
领略西域风情
感悟西域风光
天上人间

摄影：温倩

【维吾尔人民间游戏】

在农村的一些活动中，木卡姆音乐激励着参战者，给周围的观众增添活力，他们以激烈的斗羊为乐，似乎谁也不想认输。

村里或乡里举办的娱乐活动为大家彼此聚会提供了平台和机会。

雄壮的音乐同样加剧了斗狗的残酷，狗勇士互相狂扑撕咬，使旁观者兴奋不已。

摄影:文焱

高昂的音乐鼓舞着勇敢的斗鸡,它们彼此猛烈地进攻,怒目相睁,就像专业的拳击运动员打红了眼一样。

这些英勇的雄鸡由于好斗的天性而继续战斗着,它们不停地劈刺攻击,没有片刻的休息。

伴随着美妙的木卡姆乐曲,年轻的、年老的摔跤手在观众的喝彩声中运用他们娴熟的技巧,试图将对方摔倒在地。

这些传统的娱乐方式是新疆民间活动中最吸引人的项目。

SECRETS OF THE SILK ROAD
领略西域风情
感悟西域风光
天上人间

【维吾尔人婚礼】 摄影:温倩

维吾尔族的婚礼正在准备着。

在婚宴期间,客人们坐在五颜六色的地毯上。

维吾尔族是信仰伊斯兰教的民族。

他们因亲切、热情、好客而闻名遐迩。

他们用馕和烤全羊来招待客人。

在婚礼中新娘的脸被面纱遮盖着,透过面纱可以看到新娘流露出羞涩的美丽和甜蜜的笑容。

维吾尔风俗习惯,婚宴上的男人和女人要分开就坐。

此间婚礼的主持人得意地宣布新娘的嫁妆,同时一一展示各种礼品(金银珠宝和日常用品)。

当鼓声响起,新娘终于站在了宾客的面前。

婚庆之后,一对新人离开宴会。

他们的亲戚抬着厚重的嫁妆紧随一对新人之后。

宴会继续着。

　　令人愉快的节目和独特的舞蹈一直持续到深夜。

　　这些精彩绝伦的歌舞是人们感情自然的流露，表达了他们的生活幸福美满，让任何
一个参加者都流连忘返。

　　尤其是幽默节目的表演是最吸引人的。

　　参加婚礼的人们沉浸在无限的喜悦之中，木卡姆的旋律在乡村、田野、城市中回荡。

【 喀 什 】

　　喀什——曾经作为丝绸之路上的一颗明珠,现仍然是新疆重要的商业中心,它以其极具地方色彩和民族特色的巴扎和各种交易市场而闻名于中亚。

摄影:文昊

【高台民居】

　　已有 360 多年历史的喀什高台居民，融合了中亚与中原的建筑特点，民居的外墙一般都显得朴素、封闭，而庭院之内则是华美、开放的空间。

　　丰富多彩的建筑工艺和奢华的内部装饰，证明了喀什几个世纪以来的文化灿烂。

　　这些精美的帽子是手工刺绣的杰作。

　　这位妇女做好了逛街的准备。

　　巴扎在维吾尔语中是 "集市"的

摄影：晏先

摄影：文焱

意思，早在 2000 多年前，喀什就是"货如云屯，人如蜂拥"的丝路重城。

在这个神奇的巴扎里，琳琅满目的货物被欣赏、挑选、交换和买卖。

制作小花帽的手工艺人自豪地证明着一代又一代艺人们传承下来的精湛技术。

不远处的一些木雕者正在忙碌地工作。

隔壁的商铺里工匠们正在手工制作着图案精美的乐器。

一些门口摆放着做好的蒸笼。食物在高温蒸汽中蒸制，而且色香味全。

我们发现了铁匠，黄铜在他的铁锤下成为精美的器物。

SECRETS OF
THE SILK ROAD
天上人间
领略西域风情
感悟西域风光

摄影：温倩

30

摄影:文昊

精致的手工刀或匕首是男人们的骄傲。

创造精美的装饰杰作是要严格遵循传统方法的。

为了做出出色刀身雕饰,要应用特别的粘贴。

在刀具重新加热之后,雕刻的饰纹清晰地显露在刀身上。

土陶是另一种传统手工艺品。

在新疆出土最早的陶器是距今约 3000 年前的。

从墓穴和废墟中挖掘出的土陶的典型特点,是它手柄的装饰和陶身的黑色图案。

工匠们尝试创造出不同于他人的个性化设计风格。

馕是新疆人的日常食物。

它是在一个特制的烤炉里烤制的。

馕由面粉加盐、发酵粉、芝麻和洋葱制成。

有时候也会在馕上面撒些糖和其他具有保健功能的草药末。

馕各具自己口味和形状,深受人们的喜欢。

摄影:文焱

在小镇里或在城市街道上的烤馕师,为不断而来的客人们而终日高兴地工作着。

由于馕可以保存很长的时间,而且非常有营养价值,所以是商队或旅行者必备的食品。

在新疆瓜果丰收的季节,吐鲁番的葡萄,哈密的瓜,美味的石榴,鲜美多汁的杏子、苹果、桃子和香甜的梨,可口的核桃和杏仁等在喀什农贸市场都能找到,并

摄影：文焱

且深受人们的喜爱。

集市结束了。

人们赶集回家，路过的艾提尕尔清真寺是新疆最大的清真寺。

它典型的伊斯兰建筑风格，时刻提醒着伊斯兰教虔诚的信徒。

附近，阿帕·霍加陵墓被精美的玫瑰花园包围，像个圣地，陵墓里有几副石棺。

【盘橐城】 摄影:文焱

　　盘橐城,是东汉名将班超驻守的城堡遗址。班超以盘橐城为基地,抗击外侵,安抚西域,恢复了中央政权对西域的管辖,并使丝绸之路重新开通。班超纪念碑是其捍卫疆土的历史见证。

SECRETS OF THE SILK ROAD

领略西域风情
感悟西域风光

天上人间

【塔吉克族】 摄影:文焱

塔吉克族居住在海拔 4000 多米的帕米尔高原上。

在这个富饶的地域里他们收割大麦,用古老的水磨磨面。

在宽敞简陋的小屋中,他们用黏土围着烤炉制炕,这样可以使熟睡的人在寒冷的冬季保持所需的温度。

肉、黄油、酸奶、新鲜的凝乳和奶茶是他们丰盛的饮食。

塔吉克妇女是针织刺绣的天才。

她们给自己的裙子缝边,在衣领和袖口处绣上可爱的花卉图案。

妩媚动人的妇女们戴上精心制作的小花帽。

根据当地传说,塔吉克族是鹰的后代。

SECRETS OF
THE SILK ROAD
领略西域风情
感悟西域风光
天上人间

塔吉克族在庆典时会跳"鹰之舞",并且用鹰的翅骨做成的乐器吹奏音乐以乞求上苍的保佑,击打手鼓来抚慰大地。

石头城是丝绸之路上具有重要战略意义的通信站点和屯兵之地。

所有的商旅不论从东至西或从西至东通过阿富汗险恶的瓦坎走廊,必经这个戒备森严的重镇,它是供商旅栖息的驿站。

很久以前,石头城在一场毁灭性的灾难中被摧毁并没得以重建。

这是一个神圣的愿望,年轻的塔吉克新娘在饮用水或是沐浴在纯净的水中时,向苍天祈祷自己可以有许多的孩子。

这儿充足的水源是从周围的冰山流下的雪水。

分布在这片荒芜土地上的古老的清真寺吸引着虔诚的祷告者。

这些古墓群提示着在这条丝绸之路上时来时去的文明。

塔吉克族同样饲养牲畜和牧群,过着半游牧部落的生活。

夏季,这个山谷散布着他们白色的帐篷。

关卡和报信台,曾经保证了丝绸之路的畅通,现在它们的废墟已经是历史留给我们的神圣遗物。

6世纪,唐代时期成就了丝绸之路的黄金时代。

为了保证丝绸之路的贸易畅通,唐朝设立了卫戍部队和督护府。

这些驿站通常为那些疲劳的商旅和信使提供食物和住处。

丝绸之路上的这一部分曾经是尘土飞扬的土路,现在是中国连接着巴基斯坦的友谊公路。

塔吉克族有着非常特别的见面方式。

毫无疑问，塔吉克族的学校位于中国高海拔地区。

孩子们渴望知识，在学习上也是出类拔萃。

当学年结束，他们的父母为激励孩子的勤奋，在以苍茫冰冠雪山为背景的草原上用传统的"鹰之舞"来庆祝。

在山的高处，牦牛试图寻找雪下的青草。

当可怕的雪崩将要发生时，它们本能地提前逃离这里。

中巴边境在终年冰雪覆盖的昆仑山上,中国海关也位于这里。

世界第二高峰乔戈里峰在其周边,海拔 8611 米。

新疆邻近 8 个国家。

它们是蒙古国、俄罗斯、哈萨克斯坦、柯尔克孜斯坦、塔吉克斯坦、阿富汗、巴基斯坦和印度。

新疆遍地是稀有和受保护的野生动物。

新疆有许多独特的濒危动物物种,如马可·波罗羊、塔里木兔、塔里木马鹿、蝾螈、变色龙、鲟鱼、吐鲁番沙虎等。

雪豹、黑貂、棕熊、野马、野驴、牦牛和野骆驼在一望无际的自然保护区漫游,天鹅搏击碧绿的水面,老鹰翱翔在蔚蓝的天空。

【和 田】 摄影:温倩

"黄金有价,玉无价。"这是中国的一句谚语。

古代的中国人相信,用金线和玉片给死者缝纫衣服,死尸将永远不会腐烂。但是考古学家挖掘出的尸体(当然尸体的服饰是玉制成)却都已腐烂,只有骨头、金线和玉被完整无损地保存了下来,证明了这种说法的错误。

但玉能养生保健,治疗病患,并且在中国古代医药名著《本草纲目》中得到

SECRETS OF
THE SILK ROAD
领略西域风情
感悟西域风光
天上人间

40

了证实，玉石有除中热、解烦懑、润心肺、助声喉、滋毛发、养五脏、安魂魄、疏血脉、明耳目等疗效，有 100 余种用玉石进行内服外敷的治疗方法，而且被历代医者所用，效果良好。在民间有服玉治小儿惊悸，孕妇临产双手握玉有助生产等验方。

　　其实，医疗保健还不是玉的主要功能，而其政治功能、文化功能、道德功能、礼仪功能等才是玉贯穿中国 5000 余年文明史的主要功能。从中国秦朝开始，皇帝采用以玉为玺的制度一直沿用到清朝，玉器在古代已成为社会等级制度的物化。

　　文化内涵极为丰富的各种玉雕形象和技艺，比如人物形象、动物形象、植物形象的摆件、挂件及手镯等玉器被历朝历代继承丰富和发展，传至现在，起到了传承文明和文化的作用。玉是中华文明的象征，也是人们伦理道德观念中高尚品德的象征，中国圣人孔子就有以玉比德的经典阐述，并长期渗透影响着中国文化，至今仍根深蒂固地发挥着广泛深刻的作用。

　　和田玉的价值很高。玉石沉积在昆仑山深处，开采很艰难甚至冒险。和田玉的质量极高，而且色彩丰富。

　　昆仑雪山形成了玉龙喀什河和喀拉喀什河，河中蕴藏着大量珍贵的玉石，吸引着成千上万的采玉人来此寻宝。

　　和田玉是矿石的一种，内含丰富的透闪石，是世界软玉之王，形成时间距离我们非常遥远。

　　羊脂玉和河道中带皮的子玉是和田玉中之极品。

　　和田玉之所以名贵是因为其稀有和其资源不可再生。

　　玉石蕴藏在河底、河床、沼泽地和深山里。亿万年前昆仑山脉曾是一片汪洋大海，所以就不难解释有丰富的玉石沉积。

　　来自四面八方的商人云集在和田玉交易市场。

　　上等和田玉的交易是很隐秘的，较小的玉石要公开展示然后交易。

　　山玉通常是和其他岩石连在一起

的，因此，每取出一块山玉必须去掉大量包在玉料周围的坚硬岩石。

子玉则是被河水长期冲刷并埋于河道中的状如鹅卵的玉石，相比而言，开采劳动强度不大，但技术要求很高，从外表很难认清所取对象是一般的石头还是稀世玉石。

据传说，早在2700年前，有一个叫卞和的男子在山里发现了一块玉璞，也就是含玉的石头。

他把这块玉璞献给了国王。

国王不识玉璞，认为它是一块普通石头，便以欺君之罪砍下了卞和的双脚。

50年后，另一个国王却非常聪明，请来玉匠把玉璞小心翼翼地剖剥琢磨，果真一块晶莹光洁、光彩照

人的稀世珍宝显露出来，这就是历史上有名的和氏璧。

中国的玉石交易是从新疆和田白玉开始的。

据历史考证，和田玉的开采史有7000多年，交易活动也一直没有停止过。

在特别的时候，会有玉石拍卖会。

只要价格合适，商人就会出钱购买卖方的玉石。

仅仅通过观察玉石的外表和形状来断定石头的价值，对于购买商来说是非常困难的。

如果买主买来的石头不含有玉的成分，他们很少当众切割他们购得的石头，以避免受人嘲笑。

不少商人为一夜致富不惜一切代价。

这是一种非常特别带有风险的投资，完全不同于其他类型的风险投资。

购买者需要非常大的胆略，还要有相当高的玉石文化知识。

通过敏锐的眼睛，在不需要任何

技术的帮助下能说中藏在普通石头里稀世玉石的专家,在受到人们尊重和钦佩的同时还可以赚到很多的钱。

和田羊脂玉因其温润洁净,细腻微透明,如凝脂般而成为稀世之珍品,受到世人的青睐。

精雕细琢的人物、吉祥题材的和田玉工艺品,在整个亚洲地区的主要城市都有展销。

从事玉石科研、加工生产和销售的从业人员逾万人,其活动充满生机和活力。当地政府在采取措施保护和田玉的资源不被滥采的同时,也保护了河床、草原资源的完整性。

几千年来,玉石不断地从威严的冰山深处随洪水、冰雪融水流入和田玉龙喀什河和喀拉喀什河,并通过商人之手和丝绸之路流向中国各地和世界很多地方。和田玉似一泓不竭的清河,以她

SECRETS OF
THE SILK ROAD
天上人间
领略西域风情
感悟西域风光

通体温润、色泽靓丽和美好的意蕴随着历史的长河永不停息地润泽着中国人的心田。中国玉文化是一首凝固的史诗，有着深厚的文化沉淀。她以优美的文字记录着中华民族古老、艰辛而灿烂的历程，以温和的语言讲述着美丽的传说、悲壮的故事和人间的情怀。玉文化和中华民族的文明一样源源流长，连绵不断。

【手工艺制作】 摄影：文焱

绿洲和田也以地毯而闻名。

几乎在和田所有家庭里，或多或少地都知道毡毯的简单织法。

技术被一代一代地传承下来。

这些毡毯全是手工制作，用当地的有弹性的、光滑的并且感觉柔软的羊绒线为材料。

羊绒线本身混合了一些油脂，与水结合时就会有粘性（像胶），在通过挤压之后可以使毛毡接在一起。

自然染色和简单的方法使这些毡毯绚丽，并且给人一种舒适的感觉。

这些毡毯价格适中，可以在南疆大部分居民家中买到。

手工纺织刺绣图案的和田地毯质地优良，享有很高的声誉。

用羊绒和丝绸混合的纱线制成的地毯是珍藏的瑰宝。

很大程度上是由妇女做这种复杂的织毯工作。

她们精巧的技艺和专注的神情令人折服。

这些女工需花费很多年时间才能掌握这些技术。

通常她们的手艺都是从她们母亲那里学到的。织毯的手艺就这样一代一代地传承

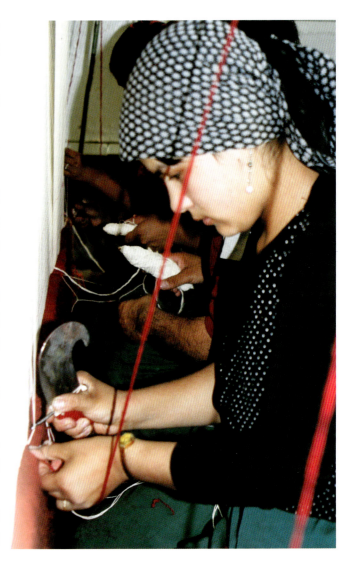

下来。

　　描绘新疆日常生活情景的小挂毯是很受人们欢迎的礼物。

　　它们的设计非常有趣。

　　游客们喜欢把它们作为纪念品买下来。

　　它们便于携带而且挂在游客远方的家里,便于时刻领略新疆的独特风情。

　　丝绸非常华丽,蚕吐出晶莹剔透的纤维。

　　蚕是蛾的幼虫,用它可以养殖成制丝的蚕茧。

　　在桑树叶里母蚕可以孵出上百只蚕蛋。蚕狼吞虎咽地吞食着桑树叶,并从蚕茧里吐出丝线。

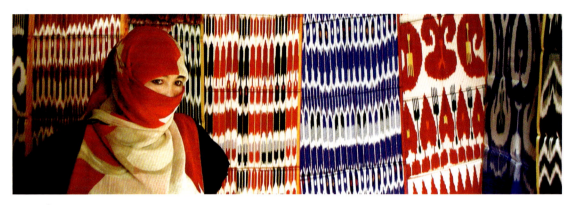

SECRETS OF
THE SILK ROAD
领略西域风情
感悟西域风光
天上人间

　　3个星期之后,成熟的蚕就能破茧而出。

　　不久,在它们成熟之前,就要被杀死。

　　因为,破掉的茧就意味着丝线残破没有任何价值。

　　茧在水里被煮过之后,蛾就会在茧里自然死亡,然后一些茧里的丝线会小心地卷在了一起。

　　在这个过程中,非常重要的环节是丝线不能被撕断。

　　之后,把纱线浸在天然的染料里漂染,染成精美华丽的色彩。于是,色彩鲜亮精美的手工艾德来斯绸就诞生了。这是和田特有的手工产品。

　　丝绸的起源在中国。

　　中亚各国通过丝绸之路这个贸易商道获得了大量所需的丝绸,但它们并不知道丝绸制作的过程。

　　几千年来,丝绸的制作过程是很隐秘的,直到由奈斯特瑞·克里斯蒂安把像冰一样透明的丝绸从中国传到了波斯后,这才让波斯人发现和明白了只有在中国才可以生产丝绸布料的制作方法和真正来源。

　　丝绸是非常罕见的,所以罗马人曾用黄金来换取丝绸缝制成各种华贵的衣服。

然而，在丝绸之路上并不只有贸易还有宗教文化。

在这条横穿中亚的丝绸之路上，宗教带来的影响胜过了其他任何事物。

随着佛教传入中国之后，伊斯兰教也传入中国。

两种宗教都变成了中国文化的、艺术的和民族的一部分。

传统的小帽子戴在妇女的头巾上，她们自豪地戴上它去逛街。

大一点的帽子是男士的，在当地非常流行。

巴扎有着悠久的传统，是每个城镇贸易的心脏。

人们都会在巴扎聚集、聊天，来自当地的、全国各地乃至异国的各种商品会在这里被买卖和交换。

这里总是有一些当地美味的蔬菜和水果快餐，比如烤南瓜或甜瓜。

时间流逝，传统的手艺被许多的工匠传承下来。

他们的手艺从父亲辈到儿子辈再到孙子辈世代传承。

中国的重要发明有着悠远的历史，而且是开创性的、里程碑式的，像指南针、造纸术、印刷术以及通过炼金术发明的火药等。

成吉思汗用他所谓的"飞火"大炮震惊了世界人民。

铜匠制出了家庭器皿，而且也起到了摆设的作用。

他的儿子在父亲的指导下忙碌地工作着。

这些手工铜壶在新疆流传了很久，而且为许多家庭增色不少。

每个工匠尝试发展革新自己的设计，使自己的作品有别于其他竞争者。

木匠正在用坚硬的木头做日常用的碗。

程序简单而快速。

很快一个沙拉碗就做成了。

使用芝麻油可以让木料不裂口且具有光泽，然后碗就可以出售了。

不远处，有制作桑皮纸的现场，一些制纸工人正在用桑树制成木浆。

中国发明了造纸术以及印刷术。

　　在丝绸之路上的中国的纸变成尤为重要的商品。直到18世纪末,欧洲手工制纸才延续了中国的传统技术。手制纸张是书法艺术家的珍藏。

　　古老的清真寺被玫瑰花园围绕着,花园不仅为可爱的舞者作为背景,而且玫瑰花被采摘后制成幽香的玫瑰油,制成性感的香水。

　　中国的新疆生产质地优良的棉花,从而使其纺织工业得到了迅猛发展。

【沙漠公路】 摄影:文昊

　　塔克拉玛干沙漠是继撒哈拉沙漠之后的世界第二流动大沙漠,世界上最长的沙漠公路贯穿其南北。穿过桥梁的河流弯弯曲曲地穿过沙漠,最后消失在一望无际的荒漠中。

　　漫长而又孤寂的沙漠公路把沙漠截成了两断。无情的沙漠一直不断地试图吞食这条花费了大量人力、物力的柏油高速路。

　　沙漠边上种植了以耐旱为主的树木和灌木的防护带。

　　树和灌木一直在被灌溉，但是它们仅仅只能暂时阻止凶悍的沙漠吞噬任何人造障碍。

　　永不停息的狂风吹扬着沙石，沙子有时像大雪一样完全地覆盖了公路。

　　似乎只有骆驼可以在这种恶劣的环境下不可思议地生存。

　　残酷的塔克拉玛干不只一次为人类敲响警钟。但现在它回馈给了我们巨大的宝藏。

　　人类坚持不懈地探险奋战多年后，沙漠终于交出了它深藏多年的巨大财富——石油和天然气。

　　从前被当做"死亡之海"的塔克拉玛干大沙漠如今被描述为"希望之海"。

　　对于能源缺乏的中国而言，"黑金"——石油是上帝的恩宠。

　　新疆现在是中国能源的重要提供者，输油管道连接着中国东部的工业化地区。

　　塔克拉玛干大沙漠除了蕴藏石油和天然气外，还有丰富的铜、黄金、铁、钨、铬、锰、硝石、石膏，用现代技术可以开采它们。

　　巨大的野骆驼群继续在沙漠里漫步，并在水源地聚集。

【佛教壁画】

克孜尔千佛洞是中国佛教艺术的一朵奇葩，也是古龟兹文化的一个宝库。

世界著名的克孜尔千佛洞是由236幅壁画所组成。

大约135幅相对保持得较完整，其余洞穴中的壁画被盗墓者肆意破坏或被贪婪的考古学者或到处掠夺的人从墙壁上揭下来运走。

3世纪，僧侣在山体岩洞中挖出洞穴。这些精致的壁画描述了来自佛教的佛经故事。

有趣的是，壁画中描述的舞蹈现今仍然存在于新疆的民族舞蹈中。

克孜尔千佛洞穴具有重要的历史文化和研究价值，自20世纪60年代就被列为国家重点保护文物至今。

摄影：文焱

摄影：文焱

【铁门关】 摄影:文焱

　　著名的铁门关建在一座险要的山隘上。

　　在丝绸之路上,这是一个重要的战略地点。

　　商旅必须付关卡费才能通过丝绸之路。

　　在元朝期间,成吉思汗统一了新疆南北。

　　沙漠白天炎热的气温难以忍耐,但是他的无畏的蒙古战士守卫着丝绸之路,并且保证夜间商旅旅程的安全。

　　破损的车队提醒商旅们不得不继续和他们宝贵的物品穿过中亚。

　　饱经风霜的石碑记录了沧桑的历史。

　　置于铁门关驻守军指挥官的楼亭,现如今是记录丝绸之路光辉历史的博物馆。

【八卦城】 摄影:晏先

据传说,800 年前有一位道士建议成吉思汗在这吉祥的草原上根据太极八卦的原则,建造一座阴阳城,也称八卦城。

太极是所有事物和生物的起源。

太极学说阐明了阴阳两个领域。

从这两个领域又说明了5种元素:金、木、水、火、土。

八卦城象征了8种自然现象:天空、地球、雷电、风、水、火、山脉和湖。

这简单的哲学观点表明了古代中国对世界万物最早的理解。

成吉思汗拟订了建造这座城市的设计图,但是他在实现道士的梦想前过世了。

早在20世纪初,一位中国官员证实有这样一个传说,根据那位道士的建议和成吉思汗的原始设计图建造了这座八卦城,也称作吉祥城。

这座全新的城市在这片广阔的具有历史意义的草原上受到了繁荣昌盛的祝福。

这座八卦城一直繁荣昌盛到了现在。

【图瓦人】

图瓦人居住在完全与世隔绝的新疆北部山林深处。

图瓦人宣称是成吉思汗的后裔。

图瓦人保留了远古的音乐和"马背上的民族"的传统。很久以前，他们横扫了欧洲，建立了成吉思汗的巨人般的帝国。直到几年前，这里修建了公路，有了供电系统才使图瓦人和外面世界有了进一步的接触。卫星电视把外面世界带进了图瓦人的家里，而且游客开始浏览这一仙境般的山区。

SECRETS OF THE SILK ROAD

领略西域风情

感悟西域风光

天上人间

摄影：张永江

摄影:张永江

　　图瓦人生活在这一片上天恩赐给他们的净土里,除了风花雪月美丽的影子,他们的灵魂不染任何世俗的污迹。

　　图瓦人继续过着他们简朴的生活。

　　他们的村庄散布在横跨密林的隐蔽山谷中。因而外来者很少能打扰村民安静的生活。

　　图瓦人不像其他游牧民族兄弟,住在新疆辽阔草原上的毡房里,而是居住在坚硬的木质房子里,用泥封住屋顶,以便它们在严寒的冬天保护他们。

　　像所有的蒙古人一样,图瓦人都是专业的骑手。

63

他们似乎是在马背上出生的。

马是他们最好的朋友。

图瓦人在连接着村庄的崎岖不平的山路上喂养着他们的种马。

他们的游牧民族蒙古族兄弟从草原上偶然地经过了静谧的图瓦村，依靠骆驼的两个驼峰作为"动物的载重负担"。

骆驼也被称作"沙漠之船"。它们感觉水源的触觉是万无一失的。无论在哪里，只要不是在沙漠的深处，水是可以被发现的，骆驼将停下来，商旅们毫无怀疑地在该处挖掘，就会发现维持生命的水元素。

摄影：温倩

【蒙古族】 摄影:晏先

当年成吉思汗率领蒙古铁骑横扫中亚,遗留在天山山脉和阿尔泰山脉的后裔如今在这片土地上过着祥和、安宁的生活。这个游牧部落至今生活在广袤的巴音布鲁克等广大的草原上。

专业的马术是每个蒙古人的骄傲和生活的乐趣。

他们在新疆北部辽阔的大草原上重复不断地和他们的家畜迁徙着。

他们饲养和训练马群,计算他们的羊群和给牛打上标记。

诞生的羊羔一直在受到凶猛的老鹰的威胁。

老鹰为搜寻猎物,耐心地在空

SECRETS OF THE SILK ROAD

领略西域风情
感悟西域风光

天上人间

中盘旋。突然猝然下降扑捉到一只新生的羊羔,然后再次升空而去。

在远古时代,在西域出名的马被称作天马。

在中国古代,骑兵需要马,所以官兵用丝绸和茶叶和他们的邻居——游牧民族进行交换马匹的交易。

专业的马术是需要每天训练的,然后年轻的骑手和年老的骑手在草原上进行比赛。

天鹅是蒙古族的圣鸟。

天鹅湖以拥有迁徙的天鹅和稀有的鸟类而闻名。

游牧部落很快支起了圆形的帐篷,为他们的大家庭提供了舒适的家。

在新疆广阔的草原上,蒙古族享受着这种自由的独特生活方式。

晚上,在会餐丰盛的烤全羊之后,家人和他们的客人围坐在篝火旁,喝着奶茶。

他们倾听着蒙古人到处漂泊的祖先在这片巨大的中亚平原上永无休止的战斗故事,在这悠远的历史中有关失败的和取得伟大胜利的故事使他们陶醉。

【箭　术】 摄影:晏先

　　有"粮仓"之称的察布查尔,是中国的"射箭之乡",主要居民是锡伯人,他们行侠尚武,年轻人大都具有百步穿杨的绝技。

　　射箭比赛在新疆非常流行。

　　射箭有着悠久的历史和传统。

　　在中亚,长时间记载着人们通过战争来掌握这种致命的技术。

　　他们射箭的准确性和致命的速度使每一个人感到恐惧。

　　当战争在西域肆虐时,势不两立的军队之间的许多血战中,射击的精确性是胜利的决定性因素。

　　如今制箭大师再现了传统的箭和弓,仿照古代弓箭的原形做出了完全一样的模型,说明了传统兵器的精致。

【哈萨克族】 摄影：张永江

　　游牧民族的哈萨克族随着季节的变化而迁徙。

　　每到春夏之交，草原上的哈萨克牧民就开始转场，人流、车队、牲畜群，从冬日避寒的低地出发，向水草丰美的夏牧场迁徙。

　　哈萨克民族是"马背民族"，世代逐水草而居，主要从事畜牧业。他们赶着成群的牛羊，追逐着大地上的春光。

　　马是哈萨克族最好的朋友，年轻人、老年人，男人或女人有机会都会展示他们精湛的马术。作为游牧民族，他们的迁徙就像鹰一样自由，他们是打猎

SECRETS OF
THE SILK ROAD
领略西域风情
感悟西域风光
天上人间

能手，他们的羊群都被圈在质地良好的木栏里。

当雪覆盖了他们海拔较高的放牧地，他们就迁徙到地势较低、雪覆盖较少的地带。

哈萨克族的营地很快地被搭建起来，为他们的大家庭提供了舒适生活和庇护。

不断地有威猛的老鹰为搜寻猎物在天空翱翔，猛然间俯冲到地面捕捉到一只小羊羔，然后腾空而去。

晚上，大家在发红的余火未烬的木块旁围坐着，愉悦着他们自己，小羊羔也享受着这一时刻。

在新疆，猎鹰饲养及捕捉猎物的训练有一套严密的方法和悠久的传统。

在神话里，鹰代表着勇气和力量。

在古代，鹰就是权利的象征。

在新疆辽阔的草原上，随着春天的降临，这些哈萨克族准备和他们的朋友一起，在低注里庆祝新的放牧季节的到来。

很快地露营结束了，驼队已经上路了。

在春天温暖的阳光下，一个个哈萨克毡房在草原上涌现出来。

大家从各处聚集在一起欢庆期盼已久的节日。

在这个令人兴奋的节日中，年轻的、年老的骑手展示他们的马术。

男孩子们骑在没有马鞍的马背上，他们飞速地追赶着，渴望超过其他的人。

据说，姑娘追起源于当时一位王子和一位天鹅仙女相爱的传说。

在他们婚礼那天，他们骑着白色的种马在月圆之夜彼此追赶着对方。

现在，姑娘追表达了爱人之间特殊的感情，同时向兴高采烈鼓掌的观众展示他们精湛的马术。

如果女孩只是用鞭子在男人的头上挥舞，

不真正地抽打他，就表明那个女孩爱上了他。这种恋爱不是在天堂里进行而是在马背上进行。

叼羊类似于马球比赛，只是争抢的是羊皮或者是死羊。典礼的操办者要将羊皮或者羊尸扔在地上。

两个队迅速地朝羊奔去，飞速地抢夺它。

另一个队的骑手追逐抢到羊的骑手，试图从他手中抢过羊。

他的队友阻断抢夺者，保护他。

抢到羊的人可以把它传递给他的队友，就像美式橄榄球或者足球中的传球。

这场比赛在飞速的抢夺者之间是场激烈的战斗，展示骑手们精湛马术。

最后谁设法将羊丢在指定地点，谁就赢得了这场比赛。

【草原石人】

摄影:张永江

在草海深处,万余座土墩墓星罗棋布,那就是草原先人的墓冢,突厥人墓前站立的草原石人,仿佛是威严的哨兵,肃穆地守护着那些有待破解的谜。

　　贯穿新疆时代更迭中的这些神秘的雕塑幸存下来,这些在马背上的劫掠军一次又一次地侵占其他部落,试图征服中亚草原和控制中国神秘的西域。

　　如今,恐怖的哭喊声成为逝去的回音。

　　和平和融洽的美丽新疆融合了多元的文化。

【乌鲁木齐】

　　乌鲁木齐是新疆的首府,在丝绸之路上曾经是重要的驿站。

　　新疆是少数民族聚居区,2000多万各民族人民,在历史发展中,文化交融,血脉连通,共同创造了辉煌的文明。

　　乌鲁木齐如今是一座现代化的大都市,高效、方便的机场,欧亚大陆桥和高速公路系统,使新疆连接着世界和中国各地。

摄影:文昊

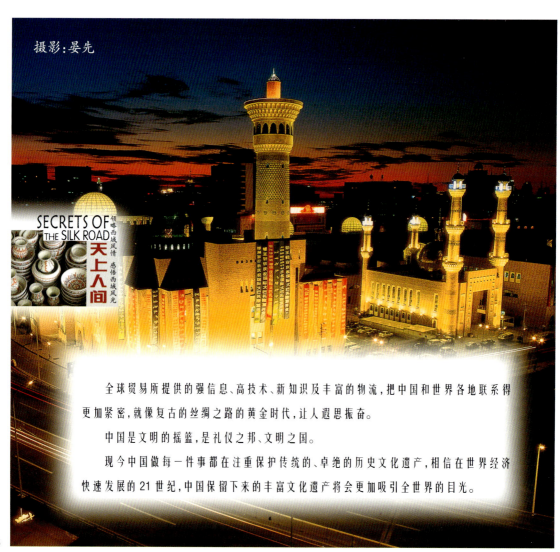

摄影：晏先

SECRETS OF
THE SILK ROAD
领略西域风情
感悟西域风光
天上人间

全球贸易所提供的强信息、高技术、新知识及丰富的物流，把中国和世界各地联系得更加紧密，就像复古的丝绸之路的黄金时代，让人遐思振奋。

中国是文明的摇篮，是礼仪之邦、文明之国。

现今中国做每一件事都在注重保护传统的、卓绝的历史文化遗产，相信在世界经济快速发展的21世纪，中国保留下来的丰富文化遗产将会更加吸引全世界的目光。

SECRETS OF THE SILK ROAD

by

CHRIS D. NEBE

Alexander the Great, Marco Polo, Genghis Khan's Mongol warriors, mullahs, monks and merchants all traveled the ancient Silk Road in search of fame and fortune.

The legendary Silk Road connected China with Central Asia, India, the Middle East and Europe. It was history's most famous and fabulous trade route.

The Silk Road was not just one road. It was a web of meandering trade routes.

A major portion passed through Xinjiang, China's largest Province. There the Silk Road split into two trails by passing the treacherous Taklamakan Desert.The two trails met again in the old trading town of Kashgar, also known as Kashi. From there the Silk Road continued over the "Roof of the World", through the perilous Wakan Corridor in Afghanistan onwards to Persia, past the fabled cities of Tashkent, Samarkand and Bukhara.

After the Sahara, the Taklamakan Desert is the second largest desert in the world.

Its ever shifting dunes continually morph its shape and size.

For millennia, the treacherous Taklamakan Desert, also called "the Sea of Death", has, like a voracious beast, devoured cities and entire ancient civilizations, only to discharge them in ruins after having buried them for centuries under its forever windblown sands.

At the beginning of the 20th Century Sven Hedin, the acclaimed Swedish explorer, discovered Loulan.

Once upon a time it was one of the 36 flourishing kingdoms in Xinjiang, the mythical Western Region of China.

Perfectly preserved mummified corpses were among the many archeological discoveries.

Modern science made it possible to re-create the face of a female mummy, now known as "the Beauty of Loulan".

Not only ruins have been discovered in the desert, but the shifting sands have also revealed spectacular vast petrified forests with thousands of silicate trees.

Streneous efforts have been made to reign in the moving sand dunes by planting Tamarisk shrubs and Golden Leaf Poplar trees, which have a remarkable endurance against exteme temperature changes, droughts, floods and fiercely blowing sand storms.

However, it is a losing battle against the forces of nature.

In the end, the ominous desert always wins and continues its ferocious expansion.

Due to climate change, perhaps brought on by Global Warming, the environmental condition of the Taklamakan Desert is deteriorating. In the mountain ranges the glaciers are shrinking, the snow line is rising, wetlands are dwindling and the desert is growing.

Unlike most deserts, the Taklamakan has multiple rivers, which flow into the desert.

These rivers wash down from the melting snow and glacier-covered mountain ranges, towering around the desert.

Of these, the Tarim River is the largest and best known.The rivers create lakes and oases in the middle of the desert before oozing away in the endless sea of sand, forming underground streams.

Since time immemorial the Lopnur People have made an isolated living, fishing in the lakes formed by the rivers, which flow down from the icy mountains.

The Turpan Basin, also called "the Flaming Land", is the hottest area in China.

Despite its scorching temperatures Turpan has a booming agriculture.

Surrounding the well tended fields like vultures, the majestic sand dunes of the Taklamakan, are threatening to engulf the protective forest belt and devour the fertile land.

Built on a lofty mesa, strategically protected by two rivers and towering cliffs, the ancient City of Jiaohe vanished from the journals of history at the end of the 13th Century.

After a long siege in a bloody war, the city was looted and completely destroyed.

Rich archeological treasures reveal the prosperous civilization, which made this city a jewel under the blazing sun.

The City of Jiaohe is one of the many ancient ruined cities in vast, rugged, beautiful and mysterious Xinjiang, China's largest Province, which only has a population of about 20 million.

Situated in the heart of Central Asia, Xinjiang is also known as the Uygur Autonomous Region.

The Great Wall and the Beijing-Hangzhou Grand Canal are two world famous man made marvels of ancient Chinese architecture.

A third is the "Karez"; a unique and extremely large underground irrigation system of wells and tunnels, which takes advantage of local hydro-graphical characteristics, based on the waters from the many underground snow-melt rivers.

This ingenious sytem ensures that the subterranean water, which is cool and unpolluted, will not be evaporated by the extreme external heat and strong winds.

This engineering miracle has a history of over 2000 years and irrigates the prosperous Turpan agriculture.

The Muezzin's call for prayer echoes across the lush valley and the ancient city, as the world famous succulent, seedless grapes of Turpan are picked and another bumper harvest is celebrated under the grape trellis with song and dance in the Uygur tradition of the so-called "Meshlep".

There are large and small "Meshleps". Typically the large "Meshleps" take place at weddings, major holidays and receptions for important guests.

Everyone dresses in splendid costumes and enjoys the grand event.

The fresh grapes are also naturally dried in so-called "Shadow Houses".

These two story adobe structures are constructed with walls which have many small holes, allowing the hot desert air to pass through and dry the grapes.

This process takes about 40 days and preserves the chlorophyl and natural color of the grapes.

Not only do these delicious grapes please the most discriminating palates, but they also produce fine vintages for wine conoisseurs all over the world.

These organic raisins are a true delicacy.

Not far from Turpan we find the Emin Minaret.

It is 37 meters high and made of mud bricks and wood.

It is richly decorated with 15 different Islamic designs.

The structure was built in 1777 by the grateful son of a king in praise of his father's wise rule.

Hidden in the so-called "Flaming Mountains", are the Thousand Buddha Grottos of Bezkilik.

They have been damaged and looted by grave robbers, raiders and archeologists, who peeled off many of the priceless murals depicting stories from Buddhist sutras.

Since 1982 these archeological wonders have been protected historic sites.

As the fierce winds continue to blow across the barren desert, we follow the caravan past ruined beacon towers.

These solitary smoke signal towers are a legacy of ancient Chinese defenses, which extended beyond the Great Wall.

The Imperial Smoke Signals were an early warning system alerting the various Chinese military garrisons of advancing marauding enemy hordes, which raided the Western Region for centuries.

MUKAM is the music of Xinjiang.

It celebrates the vibrant culture of the proud Uygur People.

The wild and enthusiastic MUKAM presentations are part of any celebration.

MUKAM is the heart beat of Xinjiang and a must for every "Meshlep"!

Uygur men and women like to wear beautifully embroidered skullcaps.

The women dress in multicolored silk dresses and keep their hair in braids.

Traditionally, when Uygurs greet each other, they do not shake hands but place their right hand on the left side of their chest, bow and say: "I wish you a good 81 fortune".

To show special respect in front of distinguished guests and elders, both arms are crossed in front of the chest.

Women have their own etiquette. They embrace and touch each other's right cheek and say "Good fortune".

The majority of the Uygurs are farmers and the country fair is a welcome way to get together and celebrate.

At country fairs Mukam stimulates the combatants and energizes the crowd.

The fiercely fighting rams, who never seem to give up, delight young and old.

MUKAM also intensifies the vicious dog fights, which are cheered by excited onlookers.

Mukam encourages brave cocks, to fight each other "an eye for an eye" like professional heavy weights.

These valiant roosters continue to fascinate the crowd with their fighting spirit, as they are repeatedly attacking each other without a moments rest.

Last but not least MUKAM applauds these wrestlers, who are skillfully struggling to throw their opponents to the ground.

These good natured games have a long tradition and are the main attractions of the many country fairs in Xinjiang.

Preparations for a Uygur wedding are being made.

Colorfull carpets are placed on the ground for the guests to sit on during the feast.

The Uygurs are Muslims.

They are wellknown for their warm and generous hospitality.

"Nan", the daily bread, and whole roasted sheep are being served to the many guests.

The bride is veiled for the wedding ceremony.

As tradition demands the women sit separately from the men.

For all to see, the Master of Ceremony proudly announces the dowry and presents the various gifts, which range from jewelry and cash to household items.

As the drum beat intensifies, the bride, at last, is led in front of the Imam, who performs the wedding rites.

After the ceremony the newly-weds leave the party.

Their happy relatives carry the heavy dowry trunk.

The party goes on, bursting with the joy of life.

Engaging entertainment and spontaneous dance continue until late at night.

These wonderful, fresh and natural expressions of life, make any celebration in Xinjiang an unforgettable, down to earth experience.

This is humanity in its most appealing form.

Neighbors follow the party with interest as the timeless Mukam beat echoes across the roofs of the city.

Kashgar, once known as "The Pearl of the Silk Road", still is an important commercial center.

Its bazaar and cattle market are famous all over Central Asia.

Kashgar's rich architecture and lavish interiors document the wealth of its merchants and artisans, who have prospered for centuries by trading and bartering in this strategically located town.

These fine skull caps are hand embroidered masterpieces.

This lady is leaving for her daily visit to the bazaar.

In this legendary bazaar exotic goods from all over are admired,　bought,　bartered and sold.

The hat maker expertly demonstrates his skill in the time honored tradition handed down from generation to generation.

A few steps away wood carvers are busy at work.

While next door fine musical instruments are hand crafted with intricate designs.

A few more doors down food steamers, made from bamboo, are produced.

Food steamed in them is free from excessive moisture, which makes it more appealing to the palate.

No wonder most Chinese families use them.

Here we find metal workers turning out precious copper and brass wares.

It is the desire of every man in Xinjiang is to own a finely crafted knife or dagger.

Traditional methods are strictly adhered to in creating exquisitely decorated masterpieces.

In order to make the blade engravings stand out a special paste is applied.

After being reheated the engravings clearly show on the razor sharp blades.

Pottery is another ancient craft which follows time honored traditions.

The earliest pottery found in Xinjiang dates back over 3000 years.

A special feature of the excavated pottery from burial grounds,　tombs and ruins are their ornamented handles and the black drawings on a rich red background.

Each of these artisans tries to differentiate his craft by creating a personal style and design.

The daily bread of Xinjiang is called "Nan".

It is baked in these special handmade clay ovens.

Nan is made from flour with added salt, sesame seeds or onions.

Sometimes sugar is sprinkled on top.

Nan comes in a variety of flavors and shapes and is enjoyed by everyone.

Nan is found in the saddlebags of all caravan drivers on their long treks, because it lasts for months and is very nourishing.

In small country bakeries or on city streets the "Nan" bakers are constantly at work to please their steady flow of customers.

The famous grapes of Turpan, the honey dew and water melons of Hami, the delicious pomegranates, succulent apricots, apples, peaches, fragrant pears, thin shelled walnuts and almonds of Xinjiang can be found during season in abundance at any market and are cherished all over China.

Another market day is over.

The farmers head home past the famous Idkah Mosque of Kashgar, the biggest of Xinjiang's many mosques.

Built in the harmonious tranquil beauty of Islamic architecture it reminds the faithful of their daily prayers.

The nearby Apakhoja Mausoleum, surrounded by lavish, exquisitely tended rose gardens, was built as a burial shrine and houses richly decorated stone coffins.

The BAN CHAO Memorial honors Chinese forces, which throughout history have valiantly defended

Xinjiang against marauding war lords.

The Indo-Germanic Tajiks live at elevations of over 4000 meters above sea level on the "Roof of the World".

In the fertile valleys they harvest mountain barley, which is ground in ancient water powered mills.

In their spacious adobe huts the beds are built around the oven to keep the sleepers warm during the harsh winter months.

Their hearty diet consists of meat, butter, yogurt, fresh and dried curds and a special tea with milk.

Tajik women are very talented embroiders.

They embroider the hems of their skirts, the collars and cuffs of their blouses with lovely floral designs.

Strikingly beautiful women wear elaborately ornamented pillbox hats.

According to local legend, the Tajik's are descendants of the eagle.

When celebrating the "Eagle Dance" the Tajiks praise heaven with flutes made from the wing bones of eagles and console the earth with the rhythmic beat of their hand drums.

The strategically located Stone City was once an important military garrison, customs and courier station on the Silk Road.

All caravans on their way East or West through the perilous Wakan Corridor of Afghanistan had to pass through this heavily fortified city, which essentially served as the gate way to the Middle Kingdom.

Long ago the city was destroyed by a devastating earthquake and never rebuilt.

This is the mysterious wishing well, where young Tajik brides bathe in crystal clear water and pray to the heavens, hoping to have many children.

There is plenty of fresh water available from the melting snow, which flows down from the surrounding mountain ranges.

Old mosques dot the barren landscape inviting the faithful to prayer.

These burial tombs remind us of the many civilizations which have come and gone along the Silk Road.

Tajiks are also live stock breeders and herders, and lead a semi nomadic life.

During the summer months their round white tents are scattered throughout the valleys.

Customs and postal messenger stations, like this one, once served the Silk Road.

Now their ruins are relics of a distant past.

This part of the ancient Silk Road was once a dirt road, now it is a modern highway connecting China with Afghanistan, Pakistan and India.

The Golden Era of the Silk Road started with the Tang Dynasty, established in the 6th Century. In order to guarantee peaceful trade along the Silk Road, the Tang Dynasty built military garrisons and postal courier stations, also called "caravanserais".

These "caravanserais" were usually a day's ride apart and provided food and shelter for weary travelers and messengers.

Tajiks have a very special way of greeting and paying their respects.

Without a doubt this school is located at the highest elevation in all of China.

The students are eager to learn and excel in their studies.

When the school year is over their proud parents celebrate the diligence of their 87 children with the traditional "Dance of the Eagles" against the eternal backdrop of the snow and ice capped mountain ranges.

High up in the mountains wild yaks are trying to find some grass buried under the snow.

Their instincts alert them well in advance when to flee from one of the many deadly avalanches which come crashing down these mountains.

In the eternal snow covered Kunlun mountains, this Chinese customs station marks the border.

The nearby Peak Chogori, which stands at 8611 meters is the second highest mountain in the world.

Xinjiang borders eight countries: Mongolia, Russia, Kazakhstan, Kirgihizstan, Taszhikistan, Afghanistan, Pakistan and India.

"There is a price for gold, but no price for jade!" quotes a Chinese proverb.

The highly valued Hotan Jade is deposited deep in the Kunlun Mountains and mining it is an arduous task.

Jade is a mineral rock, which is formed over long geological epochs.

Jade is usually wrapped into other stone formations and has to be extracted from them. It is hard to recognize from the outside, whether or not common looking stone formations contain the precious jade.

The value of jade, especially white and green jade, lies in its scarcity.

Jade can be found at the bottom of sea and river beds, in marshland and deep inside mountains.Millennia ago the "Roof of the World" used to be a huge ocean, which explains its rich deposits of jade.

The River of Hotan is well-known for its many precious jade stones, being washed down from the icy Kunlun Mountain ranges. Therefore, every day of the year people look for stones along the river's edge.

Hotan Jade is of superb quality and comes in many colors.

The famous Hotan Jade market attracts buyers and speculators from all over Asia.

Deals for top of the line jade stones are made secretly, while lesser jade is openly displayed and traded.

The ancient Chinese believed that a dead body clothed in jade pieces sewn together with gold thread would never rot.

This belief proved to be wrong, as such corpses clad in jade, excavated by archeologists were all rotten.

Only a pile of teeth and bones are left, but the jade clothing itself, made of hundreds of jade pieces, and the gold thread remain perfectly intact.

However, this has not diminished the deep rooted Chinese affection for jade.

Personal ornaments, ceremonial vessels, and delicately carved jade figurines have been favored gifts for thousands of years. Jade bracelets are handed down as Good Luck charms and heirlooms from generation to generation.

Jade stone gambling has a long history.

Legend has it, that about 2000 years ago a man named BIANHE insisted that a common looking stone, he had found in the mountains, contained jade.

He presented the stone to his ruler.

The King did not believe him, called him a cheat and had his feet cut off.

Another ruler was wise enough to order a craftsman to carefully open the stone and 89 priceless white jade was revealed.

This tale has gone down in history as one of the first cases of jade gambling.

China's jade business started with the white jade from Hotan in Xinjiang.

But betting on green jade is more popular nowadays.

At special events, stones are auctioned off.

Speculators must buy the stone "as is" and as soon as the price is accepted by the seller.

It is very hard for speculators to guess the content of the common stones simply by looking at the color of the stone's surface and its shape.

Buyers seldom have their acquired stones cut in public to avoid losing face and being ridiculed if the stone they bought does not contain any jade.

Many speculators pursue their dream of becoming rich over night by losing everything. This is a very risky gamble.

It greatly differs from other speculative investments.

Speculators must be fearless risk takers and have an intimate knowledge of the jade culture.

Men with sharp eyes, able to spot the precious jade hidden inside a common looking stone without the help of technology, are admired and respected experts, who make a lot of money.

Hotan "Lanolin Jade" is especially valued for its smooth shine, fine texture and its pleasant white color. It is translucent, sometimes even transparent.

Exquisitely carved Jade figurines and artifacts grace galleries in major cities all over

Asia.

The Hotan River continues to wash down precious Jade from deep inside the forbidding icy mountain ranges.

The oasis of Hotan is also know for its carpets.

Almost every family in Hotan knows the art of making simple felt carpets.

The technique has been handed down from generation to generation.

Felt carpets are made by hand using indigenous wool, which is elastic, glossy and feels soft and fluffy.

The wool's natural content of fat mixed with water acts as glue, which holds the felt carpet together after it has been given a special pressure treatment.

Natural dyes and simple patterns give these felt carpets a special glow and homey look.

Felt carpets are inexpensive and can be found in many homes in Xinjiang.

The fine yarns, elaborate designs and high quality of hand woven Hotan Carpets give them a great reputation.

For the yarns a mixture of wool and silk is used to fashion the luxurious carpets, which are highly treasured collector items.

Mostly women do the far more complicated carpet weaving.

The artful speed and dexterity of their movements is amazing. It takes years to master the skills these women have developed.

Most likely they learned the craft from their mothers, who had been taught by their mothers. The art of carpet weaving is handed down from generation to generation.

Small wall carpets depicting scenes of daily life in Xinjiang are favorite gifts.

Their designs are quite amusing.

Tourists like to purchase them as souvenirs.

At home the carpets will be reminders of Xinjiang's lavish splendor and magic.

Silk is a very fine, lustrous fiber spun by the silk worm.

The silk worm is the larva of a moth, that spins a cocoon of silk.

The female moth lays hundreds of eggs on the leaves of mulberry trees.

The silkworm voraciously feeds on mulberry leaves and spins its cocoon of silk threads.

After about three weeks, by breaking its protective cocoon, a mature moth emerges. Shortly before their maturity the moth must be killed,   because a broken cocoon means broken silk threads, which have less value.

The moths are killed by boiling the cocoons in water.

Then the silk threads of several cocoons are carefully reeled together.

During this process it is very important that the silk threads are not torn apart.

Thereafter the yarns are dipped in natural dyes.

Their brilliant colors and exquisite patterns, create the precious, handmade ATLAS SILK, a speciality of Hotan.

Silk originated in China.

For thousands of years its production was a well kept Chinese secret,   until the silk-worms that produce Silk threads, as translucent as ice, were finally smuggled out of China to Persia by Nestorian Christian monks.

This led to Persia discovering the fine art of silk making and demystifying the source of the mircale fabric, which until then was only available from China.

However,   the most significant commodity carried along the Silk Road was not silk but religion.

The religions introduced on this "Trans-Asian Highway" had a more lasting effect on society than anything else.

Buddhism from India was introduced to China, followed later by Islam.

Both became an integral part of the cultural, artistic and ethnic make up of China.

These small traditional caps are attached to the head scarves of the women and proudlyworn on their daily visit to the bazaar.

The bazaars of Central Asia have a long history and are the heart beat of every town.

Mysterious market towns, now buried by the sands of time, thrived along the Silk Road, as way stations for exhausted travelers.

In the bazaars goods were bartered, ideas and gossip exchanged, technologies discovered and as many as 20 languages were spoken, which are now echoes of the past.

There is always room for a quick snack of some delicious locally grown vegetable or fruit, such as these roasted pumpkins or honey dew melons.

Time honored traditions of craftmanship are followed by the many artisans.

Their crafts have been handed down for generations from father to son.

China has long been home to many important inventions.

Of these, the compass is among the most influential, as it changed nautical history forever.

Chinese alchemists also invented gun powder.

Genghis Khan shocked the besieged citizens of Samarkand and Bukhara, when he conquered their fabled cities with his so-called "flying fire" cannons.

This coppersmith creates house hold utensils, which are not only useful but decorative as well.

His son is already busy at work, diligently following his father's instructions.

These tea kettles have been handcrafted since time immemorial and grace many homes in Xinjiang.

Every craftsman tries to develop his own design to set his creations apart from the competition next door.

The wood carver is making bowls for daily use from solid pieces of wood.

The process is simple and fast.

In no time a nice salad bowl is completed.

Sesame oil is applied to make the wood shiny and the bowl is ready to be sold.

A few doors down the paper maker is slicing and cutting the bark of mulberry tree branches to make pulp for a special paper.

Papermaking and paper money were invented in China, as well as typography.

On the Silk Road Chinese paper became an important commodity.

Until the end of the 18th Century paper was made by hand in Europe following traditional Chinese techniques.

The handmade paper's texture is treasured by calligraphy artists.

The nearby mosque is surrounded by fragrant rose gardens, which not only form a beautiful backdrop for the lovely dancers, but the roses are also harvested for their ethereal oils, which are used in sensous perfumes.

Xinjiang produces the finest cotton in China and has a booming textile industry.

A Super Highway cuts across the desolateTaklamankan desert, with bridges spanning the rivers from the icy mountains, which meander through the desert and eventually disappear into the endless wasteland of sand.

A protective belt of desert resistant trees and shrubs has been planted.

The trees and shrubs are constantly irrigated, but the ferocious desert can only be temporarily stopped in its eternal quest to devour any man-made obstruction.

The ever lasting desert winds continue to blow the shifting sands across the super highway, sometimes covering it completely with fine sand, like fresh fallen snow.

It seems, that only camels miraculously survive in this harsh environment.

The vicious Taklamakan Desert has taken its toll on mankind, but now gives back.

After years of failed exploration, the desert has finally yielded its well kept secret and revealed huge deposits of oil and gas.

Formerly known as "the Sea of Death" the Taklamakan Desert is now refered to as "the Sea of Hope".

For energy hungry China the "Black Gold" of the Taklamankan is a blessing.

Xinjiang is now an important provider of much needed energy, with pipe lines connecting it to the highly industrialized East of China.

Besides oil and gas, the desert has also rich deposits of copper, gold, iron, tungsten, chromium, manganese, saltpetre and gypsum, which are mined with modern techniques.

Huge wild camel herds continue to roam the desert and gather around their watering holes.

The world famous Kizil Grottos are a complex of 236 caves.

About 135 of them remain relatively intact, the rest have been vandalized by grave robbers, plundered by marauding armies and greedy archeologists, who peeled the priceless murals off the walls.

In the 3rd Century A.D. these grottos were tunneled by monks deep into the rock of the mountains.

The exquisite murals depict stories from Buddhist sutras.

Interestingly enough the vivid dance scenes of the murals present the same choreography as is still performed today in Xinjiang's ethnic dances.

The famous Iron Gate was built at the top of a pass crossing an insurmountable mountain range.

It was a strategic check point on the ancient Silk Road.

Travelers had to pay a Road Tax for the privilege of using the Silk Road.

Broken down carts are a reminder of the ardous treks the caravan traders had to make to move their precious merchandise across Central Asia.

In the 13th Century, during the Yuan Dynasty, Emperor Kublai Khan, grandson of Genghis Khan, perfected the postal courier system.

His fearless Mongol warriors guarded the Silk Road and guaranteed safe passage for the caravans, which usually traveled by night, because in daytime the desert heat was unbearable.

The former palace of the commanding general of the military garrison stationed at the Iron Gate is now a museum recounting the bygone glory of the Silk Road.

Legend has it that a monk suggested to Genghis Khan that he build a city at an auspicious place on the grassland following the rules of the Ultimate, which consists of a black and a white fish, also called the YIN (feminine/negative) and YANG (masculine/positive) and the Eight Diagrams, which is an octagon formed of eight combinations of three whole or broken lines.

The eight diagrams symbolize the eight natural phenomena:Water, Sky, Earth, Thunder, Wind,Fire, Mountains and Lakes.

Genghis Khan passed away before he could realize the vision of the monk.

Early in the 20th Century a Chinese Government Official remembered the legend and TIRKIS, also called the "Heavenly City", was built according to the monk's suggestions and Genghis Khan's original architectural plans.

This brand-new city on the vast historic grassland has been blessed with prosperity and Good Fortune ever since.

For Centuries the TUVA Mongols have lived completely isolated high up in the deep forests of Northern Xinjiang, as farmers and live stock breeders.

The TUVA claim to be direct descendants of Genghis Khan.

The TUVA have preserved the ancient music and traditions of the "Nation on the Back of Horses", as the Mongols were called, when their raiders swept across Europe, establishing Genghis Khan's gigantic empire, a long time ago.

Only recently roads have been built and electricity has been provided, which make the land of the TUVA and the outside world more accessible.

Satellite television now brings the world into TUVA homes, and tourists start visiting the picturesque area.

However, the TUVA continue to live a very simple life.

Their villages are scattered in hidden valleys across the densely forested mountain ranges.

Some of them are so remote that outsiders rarely interrupt the tranquil daily existence of the villagers.

Unlike their nomadic brothers on the endless grassland of Xinjiang, the TUVA live in sturdy wooden block houses, with mud covered roofs, shielding them from the harsh winters.

Like all Mongols, the TUVA are expert horsemen.

They seem to have been born in the saddle.

Horses are their best friends.

The TUVA breed fine horses, which master the rugged mountain trails connecting the remote villages.

Their nomadic Mongol brothers from the grassland, who occasionally pass through a tranquil TUVA village, rely on the two humped Bactrian camels as trusted "beasts of burden".

The camels are also called "boats of the desert".

They have the unerring ability to sense water.

Wherever water can be found, just beneath the desert's surface, the camels will stop.

The caravan drivers will dig and for sure, will find the life giving element.

Expert horsemanship is the pride and joy of life for every Mongol.

The famous horses of the Western Region were called "Heavenly Horses" in ancient times.

The Chinese Dynasties needed horses for their cavalry and traded fine horses for silk and tea with their nomadic neighbors.

On the endless grassland in Northern Xinjiang the Mongols are constantly on the move with their giant herds.

They breed and tame horses, count their sheep and brand cattle.

Newly born lambs are under constant threat by the soaring eagles, patiently circling in the blue sky searching for prey.

Expert horsemanship is a daily exercise celebrated by young and old at competitions all over the grassland.

The Swan is the holy bird of the Mongols.

The Swan Lake is famous for its migratory swans and other rare birds.

The round tents of the nomads are quickly erected and provide a cozy home for their large families.

On the vast grassland of Xinjiang, the Mongols enjoy the freedom of a unique life-style.

At night, after a hearty meal of roast mutton, the family and their guests gather around the blazing fire, drinking milk tea.

Mesmerized, they listen to legends of victory and defeat in never-ending battles on the vast plains of Central Asia and tales of triumph and loss from the long history of their forever-roving ancestors.

Archery competitions are very popular in Xinjiang.

Archery has a long warrior tradition.

In Central Asia archery has been an essential skill perfected in the hands of clashing warrior hordes for thousands of years.

Expert archery was the decisive element in winning the many bloody battles between feuding warlords, which raged across the Western Region.

Everyone feared the accuracy and speed of the deadly arrows.

Today master craftsmen re-create the traditional bows and arrows, modelling them exactly after the ancient originals, using the same designs, which graced the traditional weapons.

The nomadic Kazakhs follow the seasons.

When snow covers their grazing lands on the higher elevations, they move their camps to lower, less snow covered areas.

Kazakh camps are quickly set up and provide shelter and comfort for their large families.

Endlessly, mighty eagles circle in the sky, scanning for prey.

Suddenly swooping down and soaring up again, clutching in their claws a newly born lamb.

At night the families gather around the glowing embers, entertaining themselves, and the newly born lambs join the merriment.

Falconry, the art of hunting game with birds of prey, and the training of these birds has a long tradition in Xinjiang.

Not only falcons but also eagles are used for hunting in Xinjiang.

In mythology the eagle represents might and courage.

Since ancient times the eagle has been a symbol of empire and sovereign power.

With spring in the air on the vast grassland of Xinjiang, these Kazakhs prepare to join their friends at lower elevations to celebrate the beginning of a new grazing season.

Quickly camp is broken and the caravan is on its way.

Under the warm spring sun large tent cities sprout up in the grassland.

Everyone gathers from all over to participate in the much anticipated festivities.

Young and old display their horsemanship during the exciting Spring Festival Celebrations.

Boys excel on unsaddled horses, as they chase along at break neck speeds, eager to outdo one another.

Legend has it, that the "Girl Chasing" game originated when a Prince and a Swan Fairy got married.

On their wedding day,   riding white stallions,   they chased each other on the grassland in a full moon night.

Now the game is an expression of special affection between lovers, who at the same time celebrate their expert horsemanship to the applause of cheerful onlookers.

If a girl only wields her whip over the man's head, without really touching him, it is obvious that the girl is in love with him.   The match is made not in heaven but on horseback.

"Sheep Grabbing" is a game similar to Polo, only that here the object of desire is a sheepskin or even a headless sheep carcass, which the master of ceremony throws on the ground.

Two teams rush towards the remains of the sheep and the fastest rider picks it up.

The riders of the other team chase him trying to grab the sheep skin.

His team mates protect him by blocking the rival riders.

The rider who has the sheep skin can pass it on to one of his team mates, much like passing the ball in soccer or American football.

The game is fiercely fought at lightening speeds by the riders,   who excel in their amazing horsemanship.

The rider who finally manages to throw the remains of the sheep into the basket has won the game for his team.

These silent witnesses to never-ending savage battles are dotting the now peaceful grassland. Nobody knows who carved the stones, put them there or what they mean...

These mysterious statues have survived the many battles raging across Xinjiang, which was again and again overrun by marauding armies on horseback, trying to conquer the plains of Central Asia and control the mythical Western Region of China.

Now terrifying battle cries are just echoes of a distant past.

Peace and harmony grace beautiful Xinjiang and its fascinating multi-ethnic culture.

Urumqi is the capital of Xinjiang.

It was once an important courier station on the Silk Road.

Today it is a modern metropolis with an efficiently run and user-friendly airport, the state of the art Trans-Eurasian railway and an extensive Freeway system, connecting Xinjiang with the rest of China and, ultimately, the world.

Urumqi treasures and celebrates the unique cultural diversity of Xinjiang and the legendary Western Region.

The Super Highway of global trade and technology, the flow of knowledge, resources and logistics linking China with the rest of the world is like a renaissance of the Silk Road's Golden Era.

The Middle Kingdom was once the cradle of civilization.

Now China is doing everything it can to preserve its epic culture.

It remains to be seen if the remnants of China's rich cultural heritage and time honored traditions will survive the onslaught of the 21st Century.